# How ^Not to Lead

## 250 Peer-reviewed Tips & an Illustrated Guide

Published by Unleash Press

© 2023 by Jen Knox and Ashley Holloway

Book cover design and illustrations by
Christopher J. Shanahan

All rights reserved.



Printed in the United States of America

ISBN 979-8-9862743-8-6

# Highlights

# How to Lead

# Introduction

Truly terrible leaders do not properly introduce ideas. Carry on.

# How <sup>NOT</sup> to Lead

# The Golden Rule

Always assume everyone's primary focus is to advance your legacy of greatness.

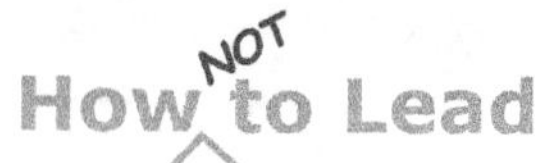


# Quick tips on Emotional (Un)intelligence

If you think the meeting might be uncomfortable, cancel it.

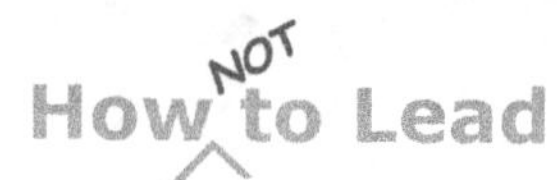

# Speed-walk past your subordinates' desks.

If someone tells you about a personal matter, back out of the room slowly, then send in your assistant.

# Call them 'subordinates' at every opportunity.

# Assume everyone knows what you're thinking at all times.

If you say hello or good morning, be sure to only say it to certain subordinates.

# Always multitask!

Answering emails as you meet with team members helps with efficiency.

# Make lots of generalizations because good subordinates will figure it out, right?

# Small talk is for losers.

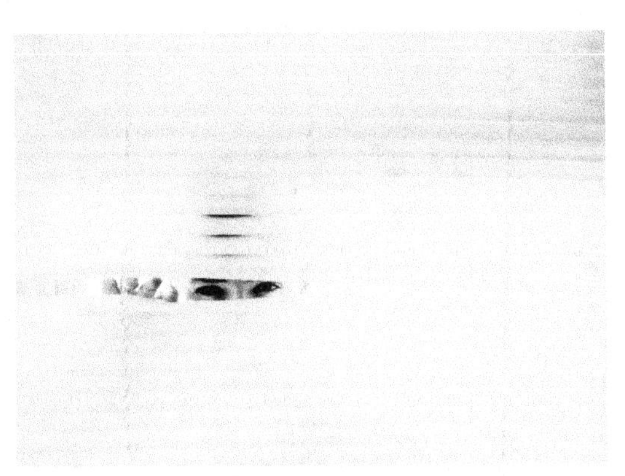

# Whenever you get a chance, hide.

# Online Communications

# Show up late and keep your video off.

Should you have your video on, keep your face devoid of expression throughout the meeting.

# Pretend your connection is bad during boring web meetings.

:(

Never show up to meetings with more than ten people in attendance unless it's to fire the bottom 10%.

# Answer all emails in two-three words (if you answer at all).

:)

# Don't use salutations. This is the digital age!

## Sample email template

**Subject**: Yesterday

**Message**: You get that project I mentioned last week done?

# How to Stroke Your Ego at Every Turn

# Be sure that you have the BIGGEST office and the BEST desk.

# Publicly take credit for your subordinates' work without acknowledging them.

Insist subordinates call you by your title. Better yet, Sir or Madam works too.

# Make it a requirement that subordinates support your kids' school fundraising initiatives.

# Hire an Administrative Assistant to be your "voice," so you can avoid any pesky conversations.

Change the
Administrative
Assistant's job title
to Personal
Assistant (emphasis
on *Personal*).

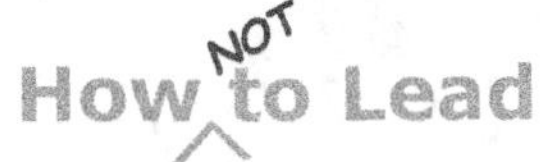


# General Best Practices

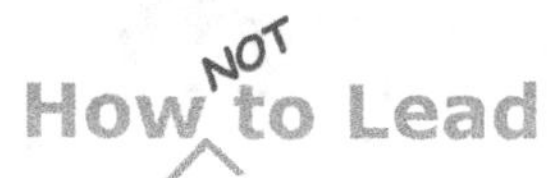



# No matter your gender, treat every woman like a threat and keep her in her place by talking over her.

# DOMINATE!

Discourage creative problem-solving. What has always worked will always work.

# Go on long vacations with no notice.

# Remember:
# Leaders are chosen.

The old adage is correct. Sometimes you gotta "crack some eggs."

# Keep your office door closed at ALL TIMES.

# Floss in the breakroom after lunch.

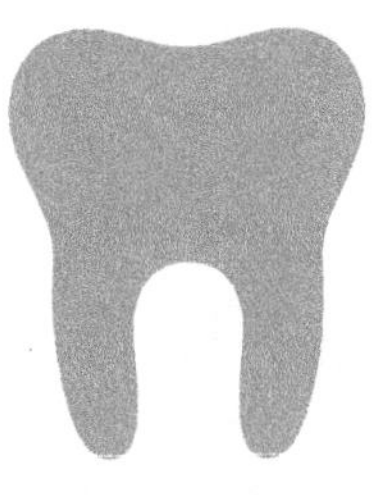

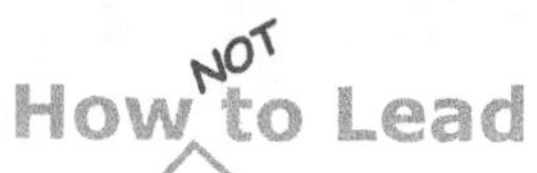


# Stay on DND.

Text your subordinates on a Sunday at 5 a.m. when you get a new idea.

# Forget to tell people when their job title has changed.

# Never introduce new subordinates to existing staff. What a waste of time!!!

Training can consist of the new subordinate reading endless corporate materials. You really don't need to explain any of that. It'd be redundant.

When subordinates request meetings to discuss sensitive topics, keep the meeting to a maximum of 15 minutes.

# Practice one-word sentences.

Send at least one joke email or meme a day to the global email address list. If anyone replies, be sure to 'reply all' in return.

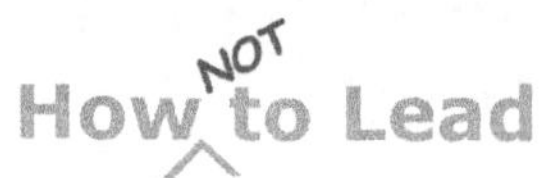


# Use "yesterday" as a deadline.

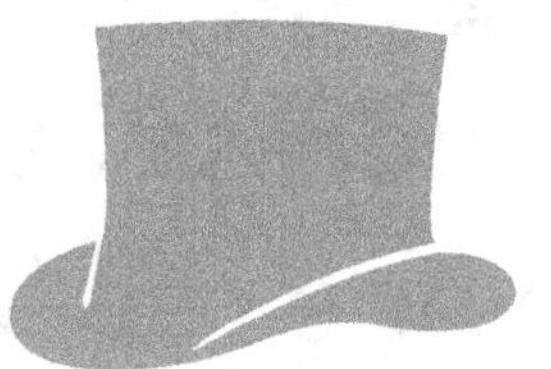

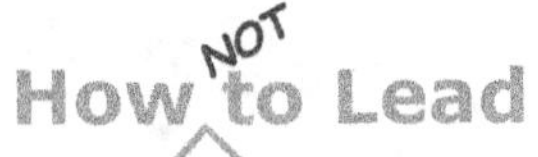


# At the Office

Smiling and other niceties are for losers.

# Remind subordinates how timely a project is at the end of their shifts on Fridays.

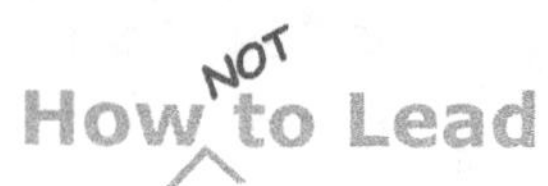

# Refer to all employees over forty as "old timers."

# Refer to anyone under the age of forty as "kiddo."

Position your desk so that people have to walk past it to enter, exit, use the bathroom or stop in the breakroom.

# Team-building Strategies

# Talk about team-building A LOT.

Throw a work party for your birthday and tell people they don't have to bring presents unless they want to.

# Make everyone read your favorite book or watch your favorite movie.

Always eat first when food is involved. Be sure to take extra helpings. And seconds.

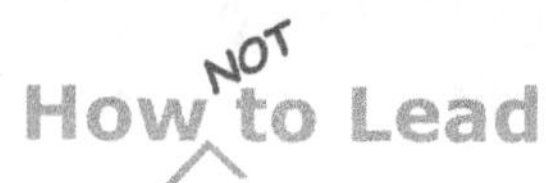

Force everyone to come to a team-building event at an escape room, then don't show.

Everyone loves competition, so be sure to make things cutthroat enough to keep the team motivated.

# Remember that people love tough love.

Teams are made up of different personalities, but the only personality that matters is yours.

# Give harsh criticism as a way of teaching life lessons.

Make sure there is an audience for these harsh criticisms. Then everyone can learn!

Never ask a subordinate how much they like their job. Are you kidding me?

# Ensure there are pictures of your personal heroes on every wall.

# Anger is a sign of strength!

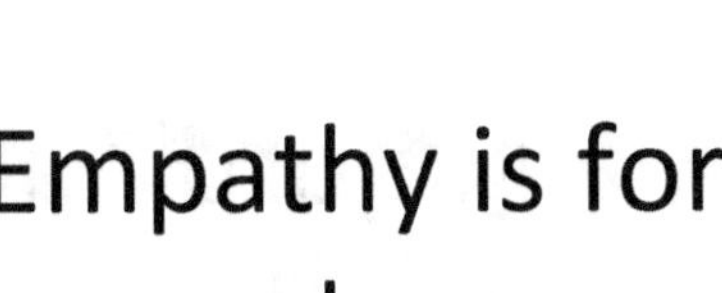

# Empathy is for suckers.

If a subordinate looks uncomfortable, tell them how uncomfortable they're making everyone else.

During brainstorming sessions, repeat everyone's ideas back to them as your own.

No one needs to know why they're doing the work, only how to do the work.

Shame is a tool—use it wisely and often.

Remember that if YOU are passionate about something, everyone is.

Send social media friend requests to subordinates, so you can spy ("connect").

# Make everyone buy a $40+ sweatshirt with the company logo on it.

# Notes on Hierarchies

# Hierarchies rock!

# Remind subordinates that hierarchies exist for a reason.

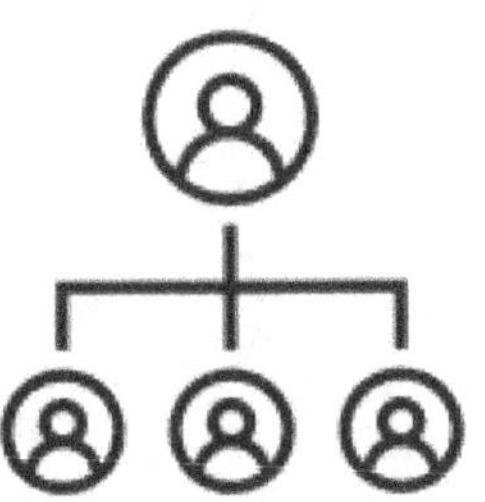

# Quote *The Art of War* often.

Talk to other bosses in conversational ways but keep the steely-eyed stare consistent with your subordinates.

When all else fails, motivate with fear! Fear maintains the pyramid.

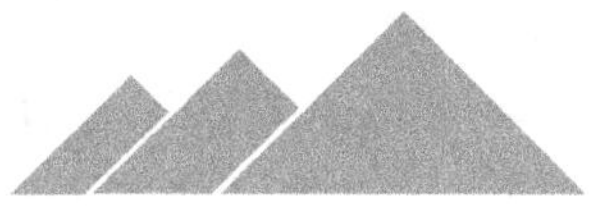

Ensure that everyone knows perfection is the only way and keep a scorecard of imperfections.

# Stand behind people while they work, and hover for long periods of time.

# Holidays are a time to double up on work.

# Disappear for weeks at a time, then show up without notice.

*(This one is SUPER fun.)*

# If you get bored with a project, cancel it.

# Make sure EVERYTHING has your name attached to it.

Pick only one subordinate, ideally the one that reminds you of you, and treat only that person like an old friend.

Remember that time expands or contracts in accordance with your beliefs, and there is ALWAYS more time for work.

# Document nothing. That's what notetakers are for.

If you don't like a subordinate, ignore them until they go away.

If someone asks for a raise, try not to laugh.

If someone asks for recognition, tell them to work on their intrinsic motivation.

# Be Hardcore!

If a subordinate asks for more work-life flexibility, nod a lot but remain quiet until they awkwardly leave the room.

If a subordinate tells you you're awesome on a daily basis, see about getting them that cost-of-living increase after all.

# Never say goodbye for the day. Keep them guessing.

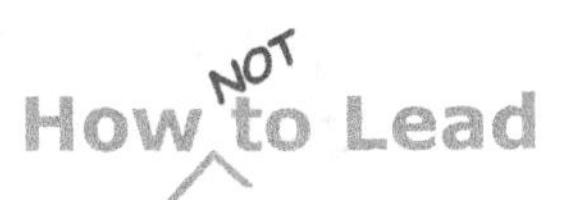



Make sure your salary is always at least 10 times as much as the highest-paid subordinate.

# Take naps in your office in full view of your subordinates. Especially when nearing an important deadline.

# When subordinates are ill, be sure to share with everyone the reason for their absence.

# Gossip makes for great water cooler conversation.

Technology was invented to monitor a subordinate's productivity. Monitor everything and chastise accordingly.

# Human Resources Tips

Remember the good old days? Back then, people could laugh at a good joke.

# Time bathroom breaks.

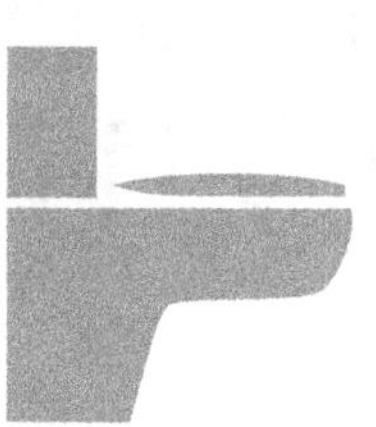

Encourage subordinates to "take initiative" by buying their own supplies when they run out.

If the entire team forgot you told them something, assume it's mutiny, not the silly notion that you actually forgot to tell them.

Everyone always has time to look at ALL your vacation photos, and it's special for them if it's a place they will never be able to afford to visit.

If you see a subordinate outside of the office, pretend you see something urgent off in the distance and run toward it.

Use sports metaphors as often as possible! After all, we can't fumble the ball. This is the game of life!

Make up a new acronym every now and then to see if they're paying attention.

# Autonomy is for suckers.

Start every day making sure everyone arrives on time. To the minute. Make sure to point out if they are late, even if it is by a minute.

Assign 'busy work' to subordinates to help fill their days. *Idle hands are the Devil's workshop.*

# Optics before ethics. Optics are everything.

# Pretend to be enlightened because it's trendy.

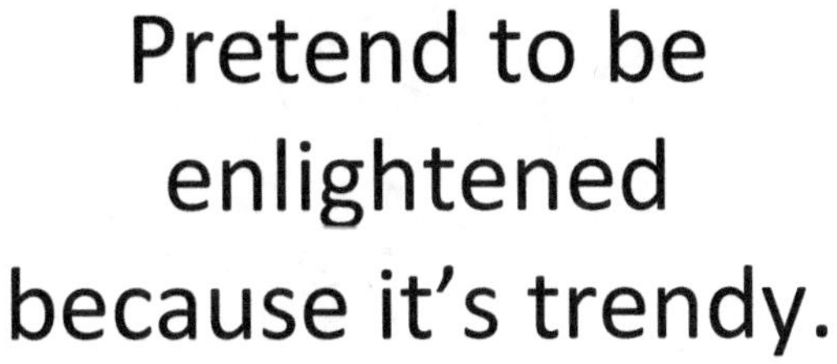

Answer every

question with a

question.

# Change is for everyone else.

# Speak loudly. All the time.

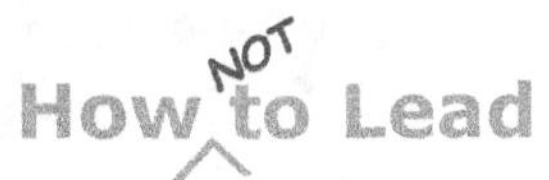

# Never apologize.

Leave dirty dishes
in the staff kitchen.
Every day.
Complain loudly
when no one cleans
them.

# Rest is for the weak.

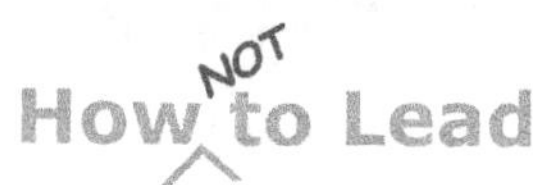

# Just pretend to listen.

Don't bother to learn about the personal lives of subordinates, unless it directly benefits you.

# Wait, subordinates have personal lives?

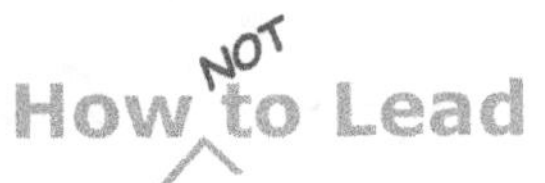

All subordinates must wear a name tag with their job description. Why bother even learning their names?

# How Not to Lead Meetings

# What meeting?

If you show up,
chew gum loudly.
Or click your
retractable pen
non-stop.

# Remind people that your initiative is a Game Changer.

Talk incessantly about yourself and tell the incredible story of your opulent vacation after explaining the cost-of-living increase has been paused.

# Ensure everyone is up to date with your dietary preferences.

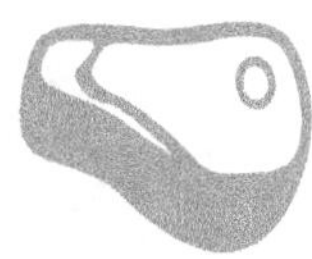

Be sure to discuss the burden of subordinates' salaries at every opportunity.

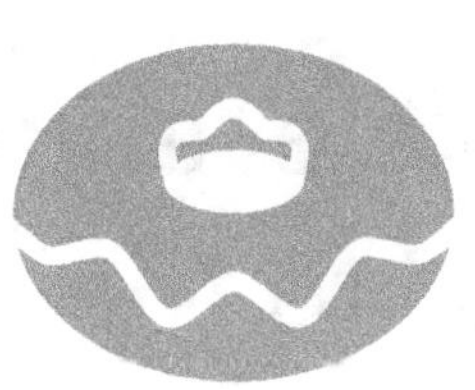

Have one of your subordinates buy donuts, and don't bother reimbursing them if they don't ask.

# Make everyone else go to the office but stay at home or somewhere cozy.

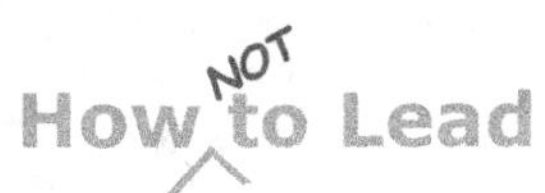


# Use PowerPoints that are at least 60 slides long.

Have someone spend hours making incredibly complex charts and graphs to illustrate your simple ideas.

# Chairs should be slightly uncomfortable in meeting rooms so that people are "present."

# Ensure the temperature in your meeting room is always a bit too cold.

# No meeting should be less than 90 minutes long.

Schedule weekly meetings for 8:00 am Mondays and 4:00 p.m. Fridays. Attendance is mandatory.

# In fact, lunch is a good time for meetings too.

# Include 10+ action items at the end of every meeting.

Pretend like you have no technology skills at all so that someone else has to set everything up.

Make sure to set up meetings to discuss the agendas for other meetings. And then have another meeting to confirm the agenda.

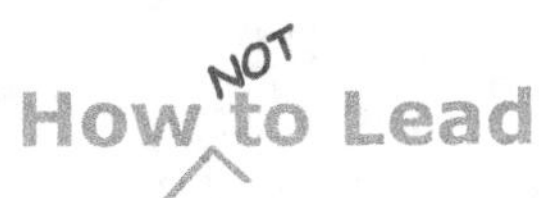

# Unpredictability keeps subordinates on their toes.

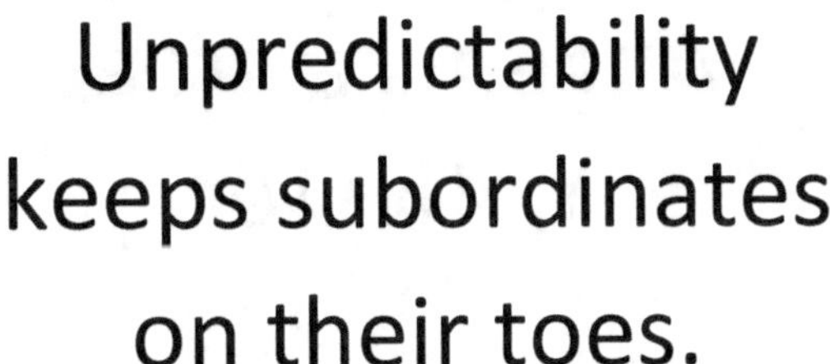

# Anger is a great motivator.

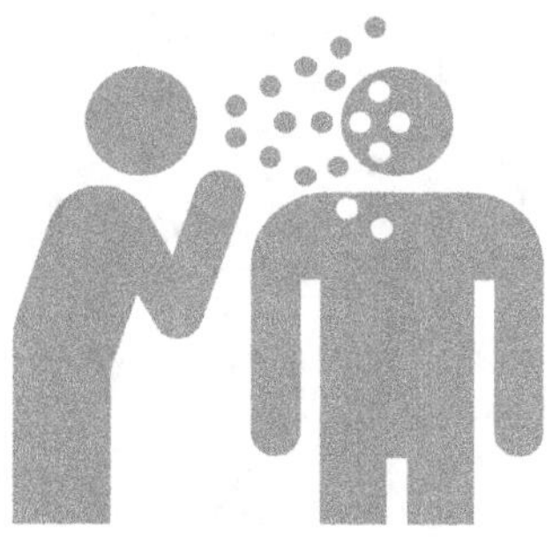

Bring a tuna sandwich, sushi or a garlicky snack to work as often as possible.

Spread out! Bring your briefcase, your laptop, your notebook, your jacket, and get comfy.

Have your subordinates meet daily for a "check-in" and tell them they don't have to schedule it in ... it'll only take 10 minutes.

Talk about your significant other, kids, pets, or siblings for at least ten minutes during each meeting, but never ask anyone else about their families.

"Selfies!" Instruct employees to post to social media about how much fun they're having at work.

# When employees walk to lunch, instruct them to make these "walking meetings." No time wasted!

Create a "model of excellence" or a mantra that everyone must refer to at every meeting. Repetition is the way to brainwash ... er, I mean, motivate.

# Deodorant, *shmeoderant.*

Fire random subordinates sometimes, just to keep them on their toes in meetings. If HR is fussy about that, just cut their hours.

People need to address their weaknesses—assign subordinates to projects they hate and watch them grow.

# Bad news should always be delivered on a Friday.

Make sure to decorate your office with heavy, expensive things that staff need to lug up to the top floor, then barely spend any time in the place.

Sometimes you just need to remove your shoes to get comfy.

# Yell, "Go Team!" or "Hail Mary!" at the end of every meeting.

# Strategize the next play to get tackles and avoid fumbles.

Play aggressive classical music and show PowerPoints of car crashes during end-of-year numbers.

Always make a point to highlight the lowest performance in any given project.

# Body Language Tips

- ✓ Crack your knuckles often.
- ✓ Flatulence is a part of life.
- ✓ Drum your fingernails on the table when you're bored.

Make jokes about everyone wearing blue on the same day, even if the uniform is blue.

Have your personal assistant buy everyone holiday gifts, then forget to reimburse that person—or to get them a gift.

# Use the phrase, "Just spit-balling here."

Have as many complicated spreadsheets as possible at every meeting to deliver simple messages.

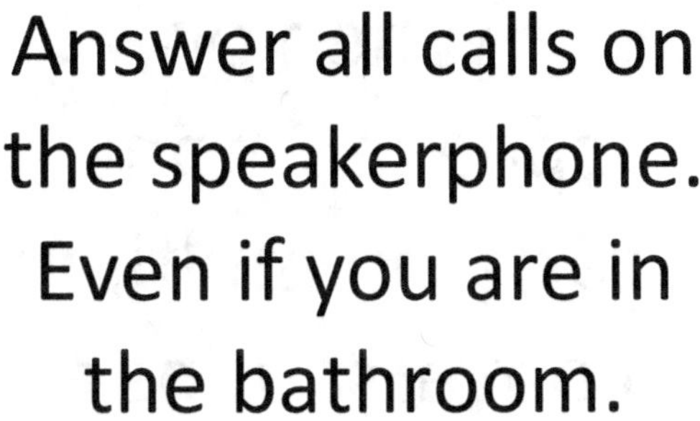

# Answer all calls on the speakerphone. Even if you are in the bathroom.

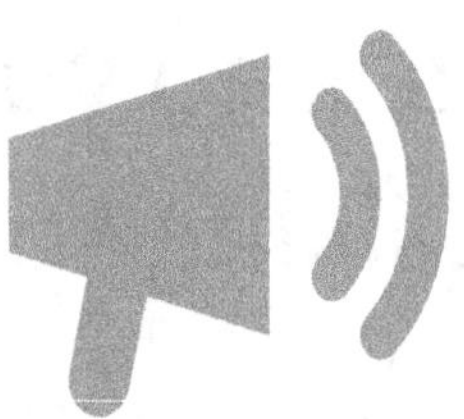

When on speakerphone, carry on multiple conversations at once so no one knows who you are talking to.

Make employees bring extensive documentation of any project wins, so you can share them with your superior as your own.

There's no 'I' in TEAM. But there *is* 'ME'.

# Use a laser pointer for everything.

Make sure the
chairs in the
conference
meeting room are
all slightly lower
than yours.

Replace all round tables with rectangular ones to emphasize the 'head' of the table.

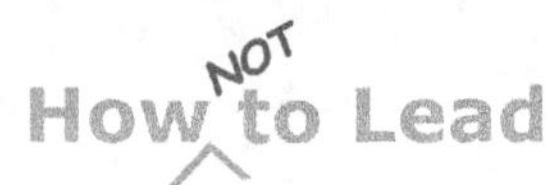


# Meetings are a great time to clip your toenails. (Multitask!!)

Insist on business wear in the office. Then show up in sweatpants after the gym.

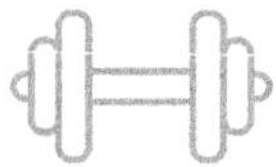

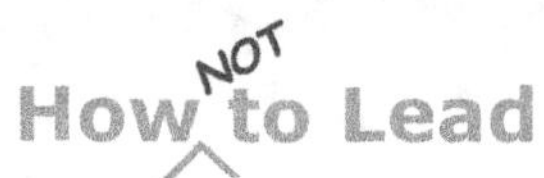


# Ignore High Performers & Intimidate Others

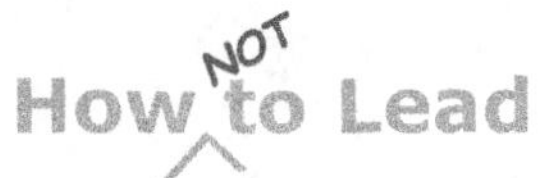


# Passive aggression is a great leadership strategy.

# Ethics, *schmethics.*

Pit working groups against each other to reinforce an '*Us vs. Them*' atmosphere.

Create checklists
for everything.
Strictly enforce
their use.

# Offer professional development opportunities only to those you like.

# Set unrealistic expectations. Just for fun.

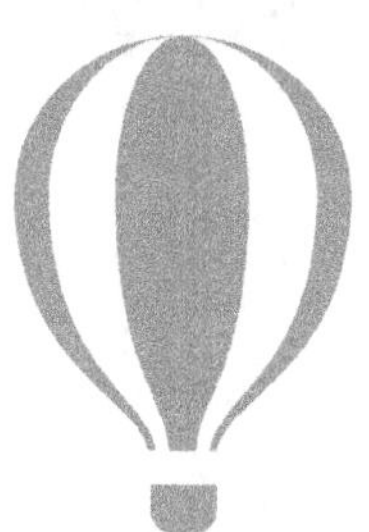

It only matters
*what* you say, not
*how* you say it.

# Never complete performance evaluations.

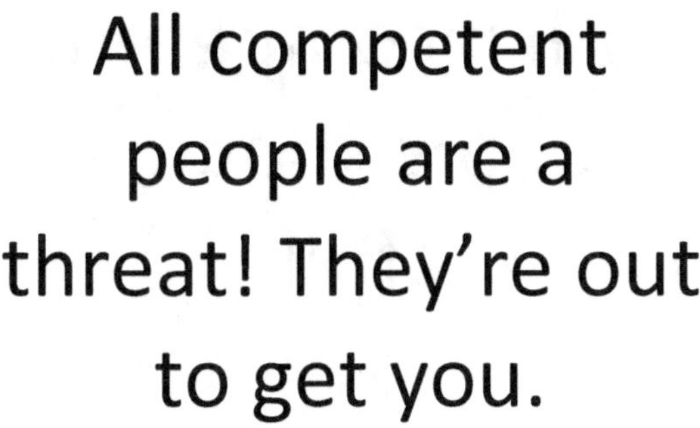

All competent people are a threat! They're out to get you.

# All incompetent people should be afraid.

Make everyone play fantasy football, then get mad if anyone else wins.

# Have your personal assistant set up your waxing appointments.

When subordinates make suggestions, respond with "well, if *you* think so..."

# Notes on Exclusivity

# Nepotism is a great hiring strategy for HR.

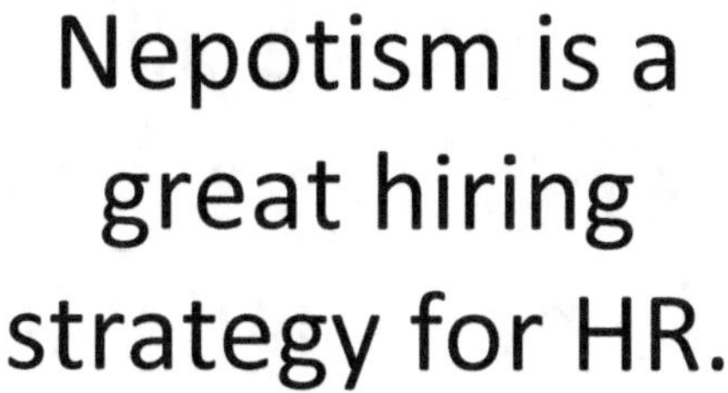

# Ignore all perspectives that do not align with your own.

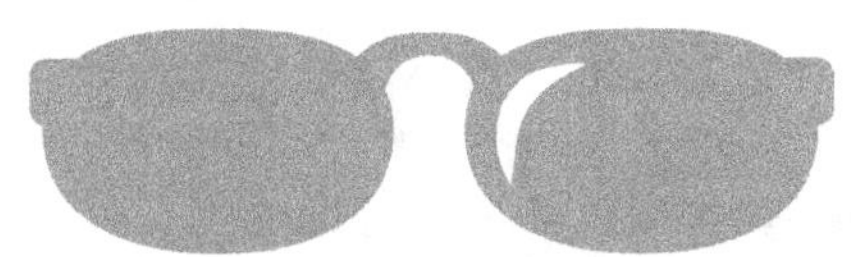

Remember, there's always a "work wife." The breakroom WILL clean itself.

Reread Machiavelli's *The Prince* during HR training.

# Only recognize holidays that you celebrate.

Regularly bring up blanket generational differences with exaggerated eye rolls.

# Treat all information as 'Top Secret'. Disseminate the minimal amount possible.

"Equity, Diversity, and Inclusion in the workplace" only applies to *other* workplaces.

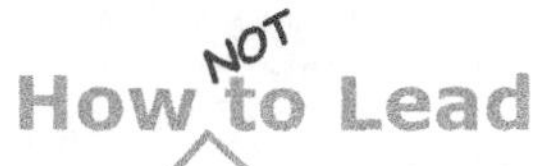


# Fun Bonus Tips

For 1:1 meetings in your office, make subordinates stand in front of your desk.

Knowledge is power. Make sure subordinates have only the bare minimum. Of both.

# Wait at least 24 hours before you respond to urgent emails.

Manifest greatness. If everything's not great, it's someone else's fault.

Delegate!
Delegate!
Delegate!
Delegate
everything. And I
mean *everything*.

# Create a sense of urgency. For everything.

There is only one way to deal with conflict: by being louder than the other person.

# Better yet, avoid conflict altogether.

# Start most conversations with "That reminds me of a time when I..."

# Insist that subordinates use Comic Sans font for ALL correspondence.

# Key Takeaways

If you weren't
paying attention,
you were fumbling
the ball.

We promised 250 peer-reviewed tips on how not to lead, but we didn't actually count them. There's probably about 250 here. Whatever. You get the point.

# How $^{NOT}$ to Lead

About the Authors:

Jen Knox is HARDCORE. She taught leadership, she's a leadership expert (whose expertise is beyond compare), and she even led a few people. If she really took off the gloves and showed you how talented she was, you'd be screaming "Hail Mary!" Her advice is to keep on hustling, and one day you might end up a true GAME CHANGER in your industry. And that's what it's all about, right?

Ashley Holloway is a self-made leadership expert that came from humble beginnings. She rose up like a phoenix from the ashes to CONQUER and now has a top-floor corner office, where she leads others to (her) greatness. She doesn't just sit on Boards, she *owns* them.